Level 3: 750 vocabulary words

The Making of the First Emperor

秦始皇

叶婵娟 改编
张 乐 翻译

MP3
Download Online
www.sinolingua.com.cn

Sinolingua
华语教学出版社

First Edition   2017
Second Printing   2022

ISBN 978-7-5138-1401-0
Copyright 2017 by Sinolingua Co., Ltd
Published by Sinolingua Co., Ltd
24 Baiwanzhuang Street, Beijing 100037, China
Tel: (86) 10-68320585 68997826
Fax: (86) 10-68997826 68326333
http://www.sinolingua.com.cn
E-mail: hyjx@sinolingua.com.cn
Facebook: www.facebook.com/sinolingua
Printed by Beijing Hucais Culture Communication Co., Ltd

Printed in the People's Republic of China

编者的话

对于广大汉语学习者来说,要想快速提高汉语水平,扩大阅读量是很有必要的。"彩虹桥"汉语分级读物为汉语学习者提供了一系列有趣、有用的汉语阅读材料。本系列读物按照词汇量进行分级,力求用限定的词汇讲述精彩的故事。本套读物主要有以下特点:

一、分级精准,循序渐进。我们参考"新汉语水平考试(HSK)词汇表"(2012年修订版)、《汉语国际教育用音节汉字词汇等级划分(国家标准)》和《常用汉语1500高频词语表》等词汇分级标准,结合《欧洲语言教学与评估框架性共同标准》(CEFR),设计了一套适合汉语学习者的"彩虹桥"词汇分级标准。本系列读物分为7个级别(入门级*、1级、2级、3级、4级、5级、6级),供不同水平的汉语学习者选择,每个级别故事的生词数量不超过本级别对应词汇量的20%。随着级别的升高,故事的篇幅逐渐加长。本系列读物与HSK、CEFR的对应级别,各级词汇量以及每本书的字数详见下表。

---

* 入门级(Starter)在封底用S标识。

级别	入门级	1级	2级	3级	4级	5级	6级
对应级别	HSK1 CEFR A1	HSK1-2 CEFR A1-A2	HSK2-3 CEFR A2-B1	HSK3 CEFR A2-B1	HSK3-4 CEFR B1	HSK4 CEFR B1-B2	HSK5 CEFR B2-C1
词汇量	150	300	500	750	1 000	1 500	2 500
字数	1 000	2 500	5 000	7 500	10 000	15 000	25 000

　　二、故事精彩，题材多样。本套读物选材的标准就是"精彩"，所选的故事要么曲折离奇，要么感人至深，对读者构成奇妙的吸引力。选题广泛取材于中国的神话传说、民间故事、文学名著、名人传记和历史故事等，让汉语学习者在阅读中潜移默化地了解中国的文化和历史。

　　三、结构合理，实用性强。"彩虹桥"系列读物的每一本书中，除了中文故事正文之外，都配有主要人物的中英文介绍、生词英文注释及例句、故事正文的英文翻译、练习题和生词表，方便读者阅读和理解故事内容，提升汉语阅读能力。练习题主要采用客观题，题型多样，难度适中，并附有参考答案，既可供汉语教师在课堂上教学使用，又可供汉语学习者进行自我水平检测。

　　如果您对本系列读物有什么想法，比如推荐精彩故事、提出改进意见等，请发邮件到 liuxiaolin@sinolingua.com.cn，与我们交流探讨。也可以关注我们的微信公众号 CHQRainbowBridge，随时与我们交流互动。同时，微信公众号会不定期发布有关"彩虹桥"的出版信息，以及汉语阅读、中国文化小知识等。

韩　颖　刘小琳

Preface

For students who study Chinese as a foreign language, it's crucial for them to enlarge the scope of their reading to improve their comprehension skills. The "Rainbow Bridge" Graded Chinese Reader series is designed to provide a collection of interesting and useful Chinese reading materials. This series grades each volume by its vocabulary level and brings the learners into every scene through vivid storytelling. The series has the following features:

I. A gradual approach by grading the volumes based on vocabulary levels. We have consulted the New HSK Vocabulary (2012 Revised Edition), the *Graded Chinese Syllables, Characters and Words for the Application of Teaching Chinese to the Speakers of Other Languages (National Standard)* and the 1,500 Commonly Used High Frequency Chinese Vocabulary, along with the Common European Framework of Reference for Languages (CEFR) to design the "Rainbow Bridge" vocabulary grading standard. The series is divided into seven levels (Starter*, Level 1, Level 2, Level 3, Level 4, Level 5 and Level 6) for students at different stages in their Chinese education to choose from. For each level, new words are no more than 20% of the vocabulary amount as specified in the corresponding HSK and CEFR levels. As the levels progress, the passage length will in turn increase. The following table indicates the corresponding "Rainbow Bridge" level, HSK and CEFR levels, the vocabulary amount, and number of characters.

---

* Represented by "S" on the back cover.

Level	Starter	1	2	3	4	5	6
HSK/ CEFR Level	HSK1 CEFR A1	HSK1-2 CEFR A1-A2	HSK2-3 CEFR A2-B1	HSK3 CEFR A2-B1	HSK3-4 CEFR B1	HSK4 CEFR B1-B2	HSK5 CEFR B2-C1
Vocabulary	150	300	500	750	1,000	1,500	2,500
Characters	1,000	2,500	5,000	7,500	10,000	15,000	25,000

II. Intriguing stories on various themes. The series features engaging stories known for their twists and turns as well as deeply touching plots. The readers will find it a joyful experience to read the stories. The topics are selected from Chinese mythology, legends, folklore, literary classics, biographies of renowned people and historical tales. Such wide-ranging topics exert an invisible, yet formative, influence on readers' understanding of Chinese culture and history.

III. Reasonably structured and easy to use. For each volume of the "Rainbow Bridge" series, apart from a Chinese story, we also provide an introduction to the main characters in Chinese and English, new words with English explanations and sample sentences, and an English translation of the story, followed by comprehension exercises and a vocabulary list to help users read and understand the story and improve their Chinese reading skills. The exercises are mainly presented as objective questions that take on various forms with moderate difficulty. Moreover, keys to the exercises are also provided. The series can be used by teachers in class or by students for self-study.

If you have any questions, comments or suggestions about the series, please email us at liuxiaolin@sinolingua.com.cn. You can also exchange ideas with us via our WeChat account: CHQRainbowBridge. This account will provide updates on the series along with Chinese reading materials and cultural tips.

Han Ying and Liu Xiaolin

主要人物和时代背景
Main Characters and Historical Background

秦始皇（Qínshǐhuáng）：名叫嬴政，中国历史上著名的政治家，也是第一个称"皇帝"的君主。

The First Emperor of the Qin Dynasty: One of the most well-known statesmen in Chinese history, and the first monarch to claim the title of huangdi (emperor); Also known by his personal name: Ying Zheng.

嬴异人（Yíng Yìrén）：秦国的一个王子，秦始皇的父亲。

Ying Yiren: Prince of Qin and father of the First Emperor.

吕不韦（Lǚ Bùwéi）：一个大商人，帮助了嬴异人，后来成了秦国的相国。

Lyu Buwei: A well-off merchant who helped Ying Yiren and later became the Counselor-in-Chief of Qin.

太子丹（Tàizǐ Dān）：燕国的太子，秦始皇童年时的好朋友。

Crown Prince Dan: A crown prince of the State of Yan; childhood friend of the First Emperor of Qin.

嫪毐（Lào Ǎi）：秦始皇母亲的情人。

Lao Ai: A lover of the First Emperor's mother.

郑国（Zhèng Guó）：韩国的一个大臣，他建议秦国修筑了著名的郑国渠。

Zheng Guo: A minister of the State of Han, he proposed the Zhengguo Canal project to the King of Qin and also headed the construction of this famous project.

李斯（Lǐ Sī）：秦国的大臣，秦始皇非常信任他。

Li Si: An important and trusted minister of the First Emperor.

扶苏（Fúsū）：秦始皇的大儿子。
Fusu: The eldest son of the First Emperor.

赵高（Zhào Gāo）：秦始皇的另一个大臣。
Zhao Gao: One of the Emperor's ministers.

胡亥（Húhài）：秦始皇的另一个儿子。
Huhai: Another son of the First Emperor.

蒙恬（Méng Tián）：秦朝的一个将军。
Meng Tian: A general of the Qin Dynasty (221-206 BC).

战国时代（Zhànguó Shídài）：从公元前475年到公元前221年，是中国历史上的重要变革时期。这一时期形成了燕、赵、魏、韩、楚、秦、齐七国争霸的局面，所以这七个国家又被称为"战国七雄"。

Warring States Period (475-221 BC): An important era in Chinese history. As its name suggests, it was a turbulent time in which seven contender states fought to gain an upper hand. The seven states, Yan, Zhao, Wei, Han, Chu, Qin, and Qi, are also known as the seven powers of the Warring States Period.

中文故事

秦始皇

童年① 做人质②

公元③前259年,赵国都城④邯郸(Hándān)的一座小院⑤里,一个男人正焦急⑥地在门外走来走去,一边走还一边说:"怎么还没生?不会有什么事吧?"就在他等不下去,要推⑦开门走进去的时候,屋子里传⑧出几声小孩子的哭声。一个女人抱着孩子走了出来,她笑着说:"公子⑨,你的妻子为你生了个男孩儿!"

"儿子,太好啦……"男人高兴地大笑起来。他终于放心了,有了儿子,

---

① 童年 (tóngnián) n. childhood
e.g., 这本书里有我童年的回忆。

② 人质 (rénzhì) n. hostage
e.g., 他成了那个国家的人质。

③ 公元 (gōngyuán) n. Christian era
e.g., 秦始皇出生在公元前259年。

④ 都城 (dūchéng) n. capital
e.g., 这里是过去的都城。

⑤ 小院 (xiǎo yuàn) n. small courtyard
e.g., 我和爸爸妈妈住在一座小院里。

⑥ 焦急 (jiāojí) adj. anxious, worried
e.g., 她焦急地等着考试结果。

⑦ 推 (tuī) v. push
e.g., 他推开门,走了进来。

⑧ 传 (chuán) v. transmit, spread
e.g., 门外传来说话的声音。

⑨ 公子 (gōngzǐ) n. son of a prince, official or a rich man
e.g., 他是有钱人家的富贵公子。

他回到自己国家的希望就更大了。

　　孩子还在哭着,那个女人说:"公子,给孩子起个名字吧。"男人想了一会儿,说:"就叫他'政'吧——嬴政(Yíng Zhèng)!"

　　这个叫"嬴政"的孩子,就是中国历史①上的第一个皇帝②——秦始皇。

① 历史 (lìshǐ) *n.* history
e.g., 中国的历史很悠久。

② 皇帝 (huángdì) *n.* emperor
e.g., 秦始皇是中国的第一个皇帝。

① 战国 (Zhànguó) *n.* Warring States (475-221BC)
e.g., 这是一个战国时的故事。

② 时期 (shíqī) *n.* period
e.g., 抗战时期他做了很多工作。

③ 统一 (tǒngyī) *v.* unify
e.g., 秦始皇第一次统一了中国。

④ 打仗 (dǎzhàng) *v.* fight, go to war
e.g., 没有人喜欢打仗。

⑤ 王子 (wángzǐ) *n.* prince
e.g., 他是这个国家的王子。

⑥ 身份 (shēnfèn) *n.* identity, status
e.g., 作为一个特工，他有着很多不一样的身份。

⑦ 权势 (quánshì) *n.* power and influence
e.g., 这个人很有权势，很多人都怕他。

⑧ 嫁 (jià) *v.* (of a woman) marry
e.g., 美丽的公主嫁给了善良的小伙子。

嬴政的父亲嬴异人(Yíng Yìrén)是秦国太子的儿子。当时的中国正处在战国①时期②，国家还没有统一③，有很多大大小小的国家，秦国就是这些国家中的一个。这些国家常常打仗④，打了仗又和好，过几年再打仗。为了少打仗或不打仗，很多国家会把王子⑤送到别的国家去当人质。嬴政的父亲嬴异人就是秦国送到赵国的人质。赵国有一个大商人叫吕不韦(Lǚ Bùwéi)，他想利用嬴异人的王子身份⑥获得更多的权势⑦，所以他就给了嬴异人很多钱，还把自己的一个侍女嫁⑧给了嬴异人——这个侍女就是嬴政的母亲。嬴政出生后，也和父亲一样，成了一个小小的

人质。这样的日子自然不好过，他们一家三口每天提心吊胆①，就怕秦国和赵国发生战争②。

嬴政三岁这一年，两国又打仗了。这天晚上，嬴政刚刚睡下，就听到有人在和母亲小声说话，他起来一看，原来是好几天没回家的父亲。嬴政高兴极

① 提心吊胆 (tíxīn-diàodǎn)
have one's heart in one's mouth
e.g., 因为害怕打仗，他们每天提心吊胆地过日子。

② 战争 (zhànzhēng)
n. war
e.g., 这两个国家发生了战争。

① 士兵 (shìbīng) n. soldier
e.g., 大门口有一个士兵。

② 围 (wéi) v. enclose, surround
e.g., 学生围着老师问问题。

③ 国王 (guówáng) n. king
e.g., 国王为人民做了很多事。

④ 皱眉头 (zhòu méitóu) v. frown
e.g., 他一着急就皱眉头。

了，他赶忙跑过去抱住父亲。父亲也抱了抱他，对母亲说："秦国的士兵①已经围②住了邯郸，今天晚上，吕不韦会送我走，回秦国去。"母亲一听也很着急，说："你不是秦国的王子吗？秦国和赵国打仗，就不管你的死活了吗？"父亲笑了，可是笑得比哭还难看："秦国那么远，谁会关心我一个人质的死活？不能说了，我马上就得走，再不走就来不及了！"母亲哭了起来："你走了，我和政儿怎么办？赵国的国王③一定会杀了我们的，你带我们一起走啊！"嬴异人皱着眉头④说："咱们全家一起走，会被人发现，还是我先走吧，赵国人不会把你们怎么样的。"一听父亲要走，嬴政也着急了，抱住父亲哭起来，"父亲，我不想让你走，你不要走啊。""你不想让我走，想让我死吗？小声点儿，不要让人听见！"父亲推开嬴政的手，头也不回地走了。望着远去的父亲，嬴政抱着母亲，小声地哭了

① 石头 (shítou) *n.* stone
e.g., 这里有一块大石头。

② 赢 (yíng) *v.* win
e.g., 这场战争，没有人能赢。

③ 抢 (qiǎng) *v.* grab, rob
e.g., 他抢走了我的东西。

④ 兄弟 (xiōngdì) *n.* brothers
e.g., 他们两个是兄弟。

起来。父亲看都不看他就走了，只有母亲是最爱他的。

不知为什么，秦国和赵国后来没有打仗。嬴政和母亲安全了，可是父亲却再也没有回来。

一天，嬴政看到门外有几个孩子在玩小石头①，觉得很好玩，就问："我和你们一起玩好吗？"一个大孩子看了看他说："来玩吧。"聪明的嬴政只玩了一会儿，就把石头都赢②过来了。看到嬴政赢了，大孩子很不高兴，他生气地站起来，一把抢③过嬴政手里的石头，把他推倒在地上，大声说："你一个秦国的人质，怎么能赢我们赵国人？兄弟④们，一起上，打

他！"几个小孩子都跑过来，围着嬴政就打。

嬴政被几个孩子打得很痛，他抱着头、闭①着眼睛，就是不出声。不知道过了多久，他听到有人大声说："住手！不要打人！"

① 闭 (bì) v. close, shut
e.g., 他觉得很累，闭上了眼睛休息。

① 睁 (zhēng) v.
open (eyes)
e.g., 你把眼睛睁大，就能看到了。

② 华丽 (huálì) adj.
magnificent, gorgeous
e.g., 这件衣服太华丽了。

③ 冲 (chōng) v.
charge, dash
e.g., 打仗时，他总是冲在前面。

④ 身边 (shēnbiān) n.
one's side/vicinity
e.g., 只要有困难，妈妈都会在我身边。

⑤ 抓 (zhuā) v.
grab, seize
e.g., 他抓着我的手，让我帮帮他。

他慢慢睁①开眼，看见一个穿着华丽②衣服的公子站在眼前，后边还跟着两个高大的士兵。看到士兵，大孩子有点儿害怕，但还是故意大声说："你，你是什么人？我们喜欢打谁就打谁，跟你有什么关系？"旁边的孩子小声说："哥哥，他就是燕国的太子丹。"大孩子一听，笑了："燕国的太子算什么，你和嬴政一样，不过是我们赵国的人质，还想怎么样？"他的话没说完，两个士兵已经冲③到他身边④，抓⑤住了他。太子丹对两个士兵说："放了他吧，不打人就算了。"大孩子知道打不过两个士兵，只好带着弟弟们回家了。

从那以后，嬴政和太子丹成了好朋友。因为燕国和赵国的关系比较好，太子丹在赵国的生活很好，他常常帮助嬴政。而秦国和赵国的关系却越来越不好，嬴政和母亲总是被人欺负①。每次看到人们欺负他和母亲，却讨好②太子

① 欺负 (qīfu) v. bully
e.g., 那个高个子的孩子喜欢欺负别人。

② 讨好 (tǎohǎo) v. curry favor with
e.g., 小狗看着我手里的肉，讨好地叫了起来。

① 接 (jiē) v.
meet, pick up
e.g., 你一会儿能来接我吗?

丹时，嬴政就会在心里说："你们这些小人，等父亲接①我回到秦国以后……"可是，什么时候，父亲才会接他回秦国呢?

三年过去了，嬴政没有等到父亲，太子丹却要回燕国了。回燕国前一天的晚上，太子丹来看嬴政。他抓着嬴政的手说："我真不放心你，我走以后，你可怎么办? 没有我保护你，那些人更要欺负你了。"不知道为什么，嬴政忽然觉得很不高兴。他推开太子丹的手，说："没关系，我父亲很快就会来接我的。""你父亲?"太子丹笑了一声，"他一个人在秦国幸福快乐，哪里还能想到你？我看他是不会要你了。"太子丹走了。站在门口的嬴政愣①住了，原来朋友是这样看他的。父亲真的不要他了吗？不会的，他一定会等到父亲的！

① 愣 (lèng) v.
be dumbfounded
e.g., 看到我走进来，她愣住了，说不出话来。

① 相国 (xiàngguó) *n.* Counselor-in-Chief
e.g., 吕不韦是秦国的相国。

② 派 (pài) *v.* send, dispatch
e.g., 学校派我来参加比赛。

　　日子一天天地过去，嬴政一等又是三年。终于有一天，母亲急急忙忙地从外面回来，高兴地对嬴政说："政儿，听人们说，你父亲现在是秦国的太子了，吕不韦先生也成了秦国的相国①。我们可以回秦国了！"嬴政也很高兴，"母亲，父亲的人什么时候来接我们？""我也不知道，我们先准备准备吧。"一天过去了，两天过去了……父亲却没有派②人来接他们。倒是赵王，为了讨好将来的秦国国王，自己派人把嬴政和母亲送回秦国。出发的这一天，嬴政冷冷地看着母亲高高兴兴地收拾东西，冷冷地

看着前来送他们的邻居们。他在心里一遍又一遍地对自己说:"父亲没有派人来接我们,是<u>赵王</u>派人送我们回去的……"九岁的<u>嬴政</u>就这样离开了自己出生、成长的<u>邯郸</u>。

少年当君主①

<u>嬴政</u>回到了<u>秦国</u>。四年后,<u>嬴异人</u>就死了,

① 君主 (jūnzhǔ) *n.* monarch
e.g., 他很小就成为一个国家的君主。

十三岁的嬴政成了秦国的国王。父亲永远离开了他，嬴政很难过。可是他现在是秦国的国王，再也不用担心有人会来欺负他和母亲了，他终于能够保护母亲了。想到这里，嬴政的心里不那么难过了，还有一点点骄傲。可是，很快他就发现，母亲是太后，吕不韦是相国，他们两个

人决定了很多事,没有人听自己这个国王的话。

一天,嬴政很早就醒了。他坐起来,刚要叫人,就听到外面有两个宫女①在小声说话。一个宫女说:"你知道吗?昨天晚上,相国又到太后那里去了。"另②一个宫女笑了,"你没听说过吗?太后原来是相国身边的一个侍女,他们的关系可不一般……"嬴政再也听不下去了,他拿起床头的剑③冲了出去,杀死了正在说话的宫女。另一个宫女吓④坏了,马上往外面跑,几个士兵听到,跑进来要抢嬴政手里的剑。嬴政气得大叫:"我是秦王,谁敢抢我的剑!"士兵们不敢动了。嬴政正要杀另

① 宫女 (gōngnǚ) n. palace maid
e.g., 皇宫里有很多宫女。

② 另 (lìng) pron. other, another
e.g., 我把另一支笔借给了他。

③ 剑 (jiàn) n. sword
e.g., 我家有一把漂亮的剑。

④ 吓 (xià) v. frighten
e.g., 你终于回来了,刚才吓死我了。

① 随便 (suíbiàn) *adj.* casual, random
e.g., 不要随便评价别人。

一个宫女，吕不韦从外面走了进来。他大声说："住手！大王怎么可以随便①杀人！士兵们，你们还愣着干什么？"两个士兵马上过来抢走了嬴政手里的剑。嬴政愣住了，他大笑了几声，"很好，很好，士兵们只知道有相国，不知道有秦王啊！你是相国，母亲是太后，你们很好啊！"说完，他谁也不看，就回房间去了。

吕不韦听了，也愣住了，连太后来了也没有发现。太后问："发生了什么事？"一个宫女哭着回答说："大王不知道为什么生气，杀死了一个宫女。"太后听了以后笑了一下，说："啊，一个宫女啊，我还以为什么事呢。相国，我们回去吧。"吕不韦跟着太后一起走了出来。他对太后说，"政儿好像知道我们的事了。"太后笑了，"政儿还是小孩子呢，你别想太多了。我们走吧。"从那之后，吕不韦就很少再来了。嬴政也慢慢冷静了下来。可是他发现，母亲却和他疏远①了。

有一天，母亲对他说：

① 疏远 (shūyuǎn)
adj. be estranged from
e.g., 他们的关系越来越疏远了。

"你长大了,我老住在这里对你不好,我想搬到雍城(Yōngchéng)去住。"嬴政不想让母亲离开自己,可是更不想让母亲生气。他同意了母亲的想法。他哪里知道,吕不韦走了,太后却和一个叫嫪毐的男人住在了一起,太后要搬走,不过是怕他知道这件事。几年后,太后就和嫪毐生了两个孩子。嫪毐身边的人越来越多,他还想杀了嬴政,让自己

的儿子当秦王。

嫪毐的想法很快就被嬴政知道了。这时的嬴政已经二十岁了，他正在准备自己的成人礼①。他问来送信的人："太后知道嫪毐的想法吗？"那个人低下了头，好半天才说："太后把自己的玉玺②给了嫪毐，让他在大王举行成人礼的那天找机会攻③进城里……""哈哈哈！"嬴政像疯④了一样大笑起来，"太后把玉玺都给嫪毐了？好！好！来吧，让他们都来吧！"嫪毐很快就被抓住了，嬴政用最严厉⑤的法律⑥杀死了他。太后是自己的母亲，不能杀，但是嬴政要把她关起来，永远不

① 成人礼 (chéngrénlǐ) n. coming-of-age ceremony
e.g., 我要去参加妹妹的成人礼。

② 玉玺 (yùxǐ) n. imperial jade seal
e.g., 大王和太后都有玉玺。

③ 攻 (gōng) v. attack
e.g., 听说他们很快就要攻打我们的国家。

④ 疯 (fēng) adj. mad, insane
e.g., 那条狗疯了，你离它远一点。

⑤ 严厉 (yánlì) adj. strict, harsh
e.g., 我的老师非常严厉。

⑥ 法律 (fǎlù) n. law
e.g., 法律是保护我们的。

① 王冠 (wángguān) *n.* crown
e.g., 国王的王冠非常华丽。

② 抛弃 (pāoqì) *v.* abandon, desert
e.g., 他抛弃了自己的孩子。

③ 背叛 (bèipàn) *v.* betray
e.g., 我不会背叛你的。

④ 信任 (xìnrèn) *v.* trust
e.g., 他是我最信任的人。

再见面。吕不韦呢，他也不是什么好人，先关几年，再让他和嫪毐去见面吧！

秦王嬴政成年了。在他的成人礼上，他慢慢戴上了王冠①，"我的父亲抛弃②我，我的朋友看不起我，就连母亲也背叛③了我……这天下，还有谁是可以信任④的？"他拿起一

把剑，把它挂①在身上，从那以后，这把剑就天天陪伴着他。

中年成霸业②

本来，秦国在战国时代的七个国家中是最小最穷③的一个。因为秦国的土地在西边，这里人少，土地④贫瘠⑤，人们的生活很困难。但是秦国的每一个国王都努力发展农业⑥和军事⑦，所以到嬴政当王的时候，秦国已经成为一个非常强大⑧的国家了。

多少年来，各个国家之间的战争一直没有停止⑨。秦国攻打魏国、赵国，韩、魏、赵、卫、楚五国攻打秦国……一次次的战争让嬴政变得越来越冷静，

① 挂 (guà) v.
hang up
e.g., 我把衣服挂在墙上。

② 霸业 (bàyè) n.
hegemony
e.g., 他终于成就了一番霸业

③ 穷 (qióng) adj.
poor
e.g., 他的家很穷。

④ 土地 (tǔdì) n.
land, terrain
e.g., 这种土地种树很好。

⑤ 贫瘠 (pínjí) adj.
infertile, poor
e.g., 这块贫瘠的土地，种什么都活不了。

⑥ 农业 (nóngyè) n.
agriculture
e.g., 中国的农业发展很快。

⑦ 军事 (jūnshì) n.
military affairs
e.g., 一个国家的军事很重要。

⑧ 强大 (qiángdà) adj. powerful
e.g., 秦国是当时最强大的国家。

⑨ 停止 (tíngzhǐ) v.
stop, cease
e.g., 战争终于停止了。

① 消灭 (xiāomiè) v.
eliminate
e.g., 他消灭了好几个敌人。

② 招收 (zhāoshōu) v.
recruit
e.g., 学校今年招收三百个学生。

也越来越爱怀疑别人。他知道，在这个时代，他不杀别人，别人就有可能来杀他；秦国不消灭① 别的国家，就可能被别的国家消灭。

秦国的强大与嬴政重用人才是分不开的。嬴政想了不少办法招收② 有才华的人。这样一来，其他六国的很多人才都跑到秦国来了，秦国也变得更强大。看到这种情况，别的国家的国王都坐不住了。

一次，韩国的国王对他的大臣①们说："秦国现在这么强大，我们离秦国最近，嬴政要是攻打别的国家，第一个就会攻打我们，怎么办呢？"一个叫郑国的大臣说："大王，我有一个办法。我去建议秦王修建②一条水渠③，秦国忙着修水渠，就不会打仗了。我们不是就安全了吗？"韩王非常高兴，于是让郑国去找嬴政。嬴政听了郑国的建议，觉得很好，就让几十万百姓去修建水渠。修

① 大臣 (dàchén) *n.* minister
e.g., 这些大臣都很聪明。

② 修建 (xiūjiàn) *v.* build, construct
e.g., 秦始皇派人修建了长城。

③ 水渠 (shuǐqú) *n.* canal
e.g., 水渠能帮助我们发展农业。

① 秘密 (mìmì) n.
secret
e.g., 这是秘密，不能告诉别人。

② 篇 (piān) m.w.
(for paper, articles, etc.) sheet, piece
e.g., 今天我要用中文写一篇作文。

建水渠很难，百姓都很辛苦。没过多长时间，有人知道了郑国和韩王的这个秘密①，说修建水渠不是为了秦国好，而是要让秦国没有办法再打仗。嬴政知道了以后非常生气，想要杀了郑国，还要把其他国家来的人才全都赶出秦国。大臣李斯给嬴政写了一篇②

文章，请嬴政不要这样做。他说，把人才赶出秦国，不但会让秦国自己的力量①变小，还会让别的国家更强大。郑国也说，虽然他建议修建这条渠是怕秦国会打韩国，但是这条水渠真的会给秦国带来很大好处。嬴政想想也对，于是不再往外赶人才，还让郑

① **力量** (lìliàng) *n.* strength, power
e.g., 那个国家的力量很强大。

① 恨 (hèn) *v.* hate
e.g., 他不是坏人，你别恨他。

② 冷酷 (lěngkù) *adj.* callous
e.g., 他有一颗冷酷的心。

国继续修建水渠。这条水渠被后人叫作"郑国渠"。有了它，秦国的农业发展得更好了。

这一年，嬴政三十岁了，他真的开始了吞并六国的计划。离秦国最近的韩国第一个被消灭掉，之后是赵国，这个他童年时又爱又恨①的地方。秦国的大军打到邯郸时，嬴政已经是一个非常冷酷②的人了，当年的仇人全都被他杀死了。当年的朋友呢？嬴政已经没有朋友了！为了保住燕国，太子丹曾派出一个叫荆轲(Jīng Kē)的人去杀嬴政，可是没有成功。太子丹反而被他的父亲燕王杀了，他的人头被送到了秦国。看着这个童年好友的人头，嬴政好像又回到了二十多年前，那时的太子丹穿着华丽的衣服，在路边帮嬴政赶走欺负他的大孩子。可是他想不起来，从什么时候起，他已经失去了这个朋友。现在，嬴政已经不关心这些了，他知道，作为一个国家的王，他没有

① 打败 (dǎbài) v. defeat
e.g., 最厉害的对手也被他打败了。

② 更改 (gēnggǎi) v. change, alter
e.g., 他决定了的事，谁也不能更改。

③ 名号 (mínghào) n. name, title
e.g., 他打着政府官员的名号四处行骗。

④ 传 (chuán) v. pass on
e.g., 上课时不要传纸条！

永远的朋友，只有永远的敌人。他已经消灭了韩国和赵国，还要一个一个地消灭其他的国家。

公元前221年，秦国打下了六国中的最后一个国家——齐国，天下终于统一了，这时嬴政只有三十九岁。嬴政对大臣们说："韩、赵、魏三个国家一起来打我秦国，怎么样，被我秦国打败①了吧！楚王给我们土地，后来却来攻打我秦国，又怎么样，还不是被我们打败了？燕王的太子丹派荆轲来杀我，还不是被我消灭了？现在就连以前最厉害的齐国也被我消灭掉了。我要更改②国王的名号③，传④给后人，让人们记住我统一天下的功业①！"

大臣们你看看我，我看看你，谁也不敢说话。好半天，一个老大臣说："古代②有天皇、有地皇、有泰皇（Tài Huáng），泰皇最尊贵③。请您称④泰皇吧。"嬴政笑了，他看看大臣们说："古代有三皇五帝，他们都很了不起，可是有谁统一了天下？"大臣们愣住了，他们小声说："没有。除了您，没有一个人能统一天下。"嬴政站起来大声说："三皇五帝算什么？我要把他们的名号一起用，就叫'皇帝'，我就是始皇帝。以后从我这儿开始，叫二世、三世……万世，永远

① 功业 (gōngyè) n. outstanding achievements
e.g., 秦始皇统一天下的功业没有人能比得上。

② 古代 (gǔdài) n. ancient times
e.g., 这是一个从古代传下来的故事。

③ 尊贵 (zūnguì) adj. honorable, respected
e.g., 您是我们最尊贵的朋友。

④ 称 (chēng) v. call, name
e.g., 我们称他为"王老师"。

① 跪 (guì) v.
kneel
e.g., 他跪在地上，怎么都不愿起来。

② 管理 (guǎnlǐ) v.
manage, run
e.g., 爸爸管理着一百多个员工。

传下去！"说完，嬴政大笑起来。大臣们听了，连忙跪①下说："是，是，始皇帝万岁！大秦万岁！"

过了几天，一个大臣说："燕国、齐国、楚国太远，管理②起来很不方便。您应该派王子们到这些国家去，帮助您管理。"秦始皇没有说好，也没有说不好。他看了看身边的大臣，说："你们觉得怎么样？"大臣们都开始小声地议论①，有人说："派王子去管理土地，这是古代就有的制度②，不这样，又该怎么管理呢？"又有人说："以前的人就是这样管理的，我们当然也应该这么做。"秦始皇冷冷地看着大臣们，说："以前的人是这样管理国家的，结果呢？现在当皇帝的人不是我吗？"大臣们都不敢说话了。李斯看了看秦始皇，又看了看别的大臣，说："国王把土地分给儿子、兄弟们管理，开始时这些人关系很近，能和平相处。可是几十年以后，他们的后人就疏远

① 议论 (yìlùn) *v.* discuss, talk about
e.g., 人们都在议论这件事。

② 制度 (zhìdù) *n.* system, institution
e.g., 这是古代就有的法律制度。

① 仇人 (chóurén) n. foe, enemy
e.g., 他们本来是兄弟，现在像仇人一样。

② 郡县 (jùnxiàn) n. prefecture and county
e.g., 秦始皇时就有郡县制度了。

③ 安定 (āndìng) adj. stable, settled
e.g., 没有了战争，人们的生活安定了。

了，有些还会像仇人①一样，不同地区之间还可能发生战争。所以，不如把各个地区设置成郡县②，统一派人管理。对于王子们，只要给他们钱就好，不要分给他们土地。这样他们就不会想着背叛您，天下也才能安定③啊。"秦始皇笑了，说："好！李斯说得对，就这么办！"就这样，秦始皇把全国分成三十六个郡县，由中央①统一管理。这个制度后来一直沿用②了两千年。

郡县制度建立③之后，秦始皇十分满意，可是他总觉得还有什么问题。一天早上，他把李斯找来，对他说："李斯，郡县制度虽然建立了，可是楚地的人还是说楚国的话，写楚国的字，用楚国的钱；齐地的人还是说齐国的话，写齐国的字，用齐国的钱……我总觉得有什么地方不对。你怎么看？"李斯低下头，想了想，说："皇上，您想得很对。现在各地的人都像以前一样，

① 中央 (zhōngyāng) n.
central government, center
e.g., 中央政府颁布了新的规定。

② 沿用 (yányòng) v.
continue to use
e.g., 这个制度一直沿用到现在。

③ 建立 (jiànlì) v.
establish, found
e.g., 他们建立了最早的法律制度。

① 高祖母 (gāozǔmǔ) n. (paternal) great-great-grandmother
e.g., 高祖母年轻时很美丽。

② 药方 (yàofāng) n. prescription
e.g., 他病了，大夫给他开了一个药方。

③ 文字 (wénzì) n. script, writing
e.g., 我不认识这种文字。

④ 书同文，车同轨 (shū tóng wén, chē tóng guǐ) standardize script and the width between wheels, a phrase used as a metaphor for the unification of a country
e.g., "书同文，车同轨"是秦始皇管理国家的重要举措。

⑤ 口音 (kǒuyīn) n. accent
e.g., 他说英语有很重的口音。

这样我们不好管理，人们也会很不方便。""是呀，"秦始皇说，"我曾听父亲说过，高祖母①刚从楚国来到秦国时，拿着楚国的大夫写的药方②去买药，可是因为秦国的大夫看不懂楚国的文字③，钱也不一样，差点儿没有买到药。如果只是国家统一管理了，文字、钱这些东西不统一，那人心也很难统一啊。""对！书同文，车同轨④，国家才能真正统一。"李斯认真地说。秦始皇大笑起来，说："好，好，这件事就交给你去办。"从此，全国的文字统一了，各个地方的人写的文字都一样，就算是不同地方的人们说话口音⑤不

一样,可是只要一看文字就能明白,文化的交流更顺畅①了;而钱和度量衡②统一之后,各个地方的人做买卖也方便多了,经济③发展得更快了。

秦始皇之死

国家统一了,新的制度建立了,老百姓的生活比以前好了,可还是有很

① 顺畅 (shùnchàng) adj. smooth
e.g., 她用英语演讲,意思表达得很顺畅。

② 度量衡 (dùliànhéng) n. weights and measures
e.g., 这几个地方的度量衡不统一,买东西很不方便。

③ 经济 (jīngjì) n. economy
e.g., 这里的经济发展很快。

多人不喜欢秦始皇和新的制度。一天,士兵们抓到一个到处说秦始皇要死的人,把他带来见皇帝。秦始皇问他:"听说你在外面说了很多要我死的话,你为什么这样做?"那个人看着秦始皇说:"你的法律太严酷,老百姓都没有办法活下去了。不是我说你

要死，你去外面听听，大家都希望你死！"大臣们吓坏了，连忙说："皇帝万岁！"那个人笑了，"哈哈哈，没有人能活一万岁，总有一天你会死，人们会忘了你！"说完，他就自杀①了。

秦始皇担心了，他统一了国家，建立了这么伟大②的功业，将来的人们会忘了他吗？不行，当然不行！他开始外出巡游③，到各个地方去走走、看看。每到一个地方，他就让大臣为自己立碑④书写功绩，他要让所有的人知道自己，记得自己。有个叫徐福(Xú Fú)的人来对秦始皇说："皇上，东海有三座仙⑤

① 自杀 (zìshā) v. commit suicide
e.g., 他的姐姐自杀了。

② 伟大 (wěidà) adj. great
e.g., 秦始皇是一个伟大的皇帝。

③ 巡游 (xúnyóu) v. travel around, patrol
e.g., 古代的皇帝喜欢到处巡游。

④ 碑 (bēi) n. stele
e.g., 公园里有一块古代的石碑。

⑤ 仙 (xiān) n. immortal
e.g., 故事里的人后来都成了仙。

山，那里住着仙人。如果找到他们，跟他们要一些仙药，您吃了就能永远不老、不死。"秦始皇听了非常高兴，对徐福说："快去给我找药，你需要什么，我都可以给你。"徐福笑着说："我什么都不要，我只要带着一千五百个男孩子、一千五百个女孩子，让他

们跟着我一起坐船去就可以。"秦始皇马上让人给徐福准备了大船，让他带着许多人和钱，到东海找仙人去了。

一个叫卢生(Lúshēng)的人知道了这件事，也说自己能给秦始皇找到长生不老的药。秦始皇很高兴，给了他很多钱。卢生还告诉秦始皇，他看到一本书上说北方的匈奴①会消灭秦。难道自己打下来的天下会被匈奴抢走吗？秦始皇更担心了，他派②将军蒙恬带着三十万大军，到北方去打匈奴；又派出无数的百姓去修筑③长城，用来抵挡④匈奴的进攻。修筑长城的过程非常辛苦，有近十万人死在了

① 匈奴 (Xiōngnú) n. Xiongnu
e.g., 匈奴人大部分生活在大草原上。

② 派 (pài) v. send, dispatch
e.g., 老师派我去买一些吃的。

③ 修筑 (xiūzhù) v. build, construct
e.g., 公司要在这里修筑一座大楼。

④ 抵挡 (dǐdǎng) v. keep off, ward off, withstand
e.g., 士兵把敌人抵挡住了。

那里。但是,长城修建好以后,可以把敌人挡在外面,很好地保护中国的土地和百姓,这是一件非常伟大的事。

过了几年,有一些读书人说新制度不好,还是原来的制度好。李斯对秦始皇说:"您建立的功业,哪一个国君都比不上。那些读书人什么都不懂，只知道读死书。不如派人把别的国家的书都烧①了，只留下秦国的书和医学②、农学③的书，这样就没有人说新制度不好了。"秦始皇同意了。

去找仙人的徐福一直都没有回来，找长生不老药的卢生也跑了。秦始皇非常生气，这些人拿了他那么多的钱，到头来却还是背叛了他！于是，他派人把那些欺骗④和反对他的人都抓起来，把他们全都活埋了。秦始皇的大儿子扶苏说："天下刚刚安定，您的法律这样严厉，百姓们恐怕要反对您了。"秦始皇听了这话，非常生气，

① 烧 (shāo) *v.* burn
e.g., 他把我的书全都烧了。

② 医学 (yīxué) *n.* medical science
e.g., 中国古代的医学发展很快。

③ 农学 (nóngxué) *n.* agricultural sciences
e.g., 他不喜欢看农学方面的书。

④ 欺骗 (qīpiàn) *v.* deceive, cheat
e.g., 我这么相信你，你却欺骗我！

① 刺客 (cìkè) *n.*
assassin
e.g., 刺客被士兵包围了。

② 铁锤 (tiěchuí) *n.*
iron hammer
e.g., 他来的时候带了一把大铁锤。

把扶苏赶去了遥远的北方。

扶苏说得没有错,想要秦始皇死的人越来越多。秦始皇第三次出游时,在武阳(Wúyáng)的博浪沙(Bólàngshā)遇上了刺客①。刺客用大铁锤②打中了一辆车,坐在车里的人全都被打死了。因为秦始皇坐在别的车里,所以没

有被杀死。很快，又有人发现一块从天上落下来的石头，石头上有"始皇帝死"这样的字。人们都说，这是上天生气了，要让秦始皇死。秦始皇不信，他想：字一定是有人刻①上去的。他派人把石头附近的人都抓来，问是谁做的，可是没有人知道。最后，这些人都被秦始皇杀了。没过多久，又有人在路上对秦始皇的大臣说："帮我告诉秦始皇，今年'祖龙'死。"说完之后，那人就不见了。以前听到这样的话，秦始皇从不相信。但是这一次，他没有再说什么，过了好一会儿才说："'祖龙'应该就是我吧。"

① 刻（kè）v. carve
e.g., 他在石头上刻了几个字。

① 咸阳（Xiányáng）pn.
Xianyang (capital of the Qin Dynasty)
e.g., 咸阳是秦朝的都城。

秦始皇知道自己的身体不如以前了，这份功业最后还是要传给别人的。在第五次巡游的路上，他得了重病。秦始皇写了一封信给大儿子扶苏，信中说："我要死了，你回咸阳①来吧，我死以后，由你来做皇帝。"可是这封信还没送出去，就被秦始皇身边的大臣赵高拿走了。赵高以前是秦始皇的儿子胡亥的老师，他当然希望胡亥能当上皇帝。夏季的一天，秦始皇死在了沙丘(Shāqiū)平台(Píngtái)。李斯担心人们知道秦始皇死在路上，会有叛乱，就没有对外说出这件事，只有很少的几个人知道。为了不被人发现，他们每天都让人给秦始皇的车里送饭，让人们以为他还活着。赵高和李斯烧掉了秦始皇给扶苏的信，重新①写了一封，让扶苏和蒙恬自杀。扶苏和蒙恬真的上当了。

那时正是一年中最热的时候，秦始皇的尸体②在车里发出臭味③，李斯和赵高怕人们发现，就在每

① 重新 (chóngxīn) *adv.* again, anew
e.g., 我把书重新看了一遍。

② 尸体 (shītǐ) *n.* corpse
e.g., 人死了，尸体一般埋在土里。

③ 臭味 (chòuwèi) *n.* stench, foul odor
e.g., 房间有一种臭味。

① 鲍鱼 (bàoyú) n. stinky fish (in ancient time), abalone (now)
e.g., 他不喜欢吃鲍鱼。

② 反抗 (fǎnkàng) v. fight against, rebel against, resist
e.g., 她是个懦弱的人，不懂得反抗。

③ 残暴 (cánbào) adj. cruel, ruthless
e.g., 他是一个残暴的君主。

④ 否认 (fǒurèn) v. deny
e.g., 他的成绩谁也不能否认。

⑤ 著名 (zhùmíng) adj. famous, celebrated
e.g., 这是一本著名的小说。

⑥ 政治家 (zhèngzhìjiā) n. statesman
e.g., 中国历史上有很多伟大的政治家。

⑦ 改革家 (gǎigéjiā) n. reformer
e.g., 改革家总是很辛苦的。

辆车里都放上鲍鱼①。车队经过的时候，大家都觉得很臭，可是不知道是什么东西发出的臭味。一直到了咸阳，李斯才告诉人们秦始皇死了。胡亥成了秦朝的第二个皇帝，他的法律比秦始皇还要严酷。人们没法忍受了，一次又一次地反抗②，秦很快就灭亡了。

后人大多觉得秦始皇是一个残暴③的人，但谁也不能否认④，他是中国历史上最著名⑤的政治家⑥、改革家⑦，是他第一次统一了中国，统一了文字和度量衡。秦王朝虽然只存在了15年，可是秦始皇建立的皇帝制度在中国存在了

两千多年。他统一的文字,成为连接中国各地、各民族①的纽带②。他下令修建的长城,多次为中原地区抵挡外来的敌人,直到今天,它都被全世界称为伟大的奇迹③。秦始皇对中国历史的影响④,到今天都没有停止。

① 民族 (mínzú) *n.*
nation, ethnic group
e.g., 中国文化是中华民族的骄傲。

② 纽带 (niǔdài) *n.*
bond, link
e.g., 孩子是连接父母感情的纽带。

③ 奇迹 (qíjì) *n.*
miracle, wonder
e.g., 长城是伟大的奇迹。

④ 影响 (yǐngxiǎng) *v.*
influence
e.g., 这个制度影响了中国几千年。

English Version

The Making of the First Emperor

Born a Hostage

One day in 259 BC, a man was anxiously pacing up and down in a small courtyard in Handan, capital of the State of Zhao. "Why is she still in labor?" he said to himself. "Is there anything wrong?" Tired of waiting, he pushed open a door and was going to enter a room, but at that very moment, cries of a baby could be heard from the room. A woman walked out holding a bady and said to the man with a smile, "Master, your wife gave birth to a boy!"

"A boy, that's great…" The man laughed heartily. He was relieved. A son could lend him a greater opportunity to return to his home country.

The boy kept crying. "Master," the woman said, "please give your son a name." The man thought for a while and said, "His given name will be Zheng. I will call him Ying Zheng."

This baby named Ying Zheng later became the First Emperor of the Qin Dynasty, the first emperor in Chinese history.

Ying Zheng's father was Ying Yiren, the son of the crown prince of the Qin State. At that time, China was not a unified country. It was the Warring States Period (475-221 BC) during which many states, big and small, coexisted. The State of Qin was one of these states. It was a time of war. Different states fought wars and then made peace for only a few years. In the attempt to avoid war, many states would send their princes or dukes to other countries as hostages. Ying Yiren, Ying Zheng's father, was sent to the State of Zhao as a hostage. In Zhao, there was a rich merchant named Lyu Buwei. He wanted to use Ying Yiren as leverage for more power, so he gave lots of money to Yiren and even married one of his maids to him. Later, the maid gave birth to Ying Zheng. Ying Zheng became a hostage, just like his father, at birth. It was not easy to live under the enemy's roof. They lived in fear of a war between the two states.

A war broke out when Ying Zheng turned three years old. One evening, Ying Zheng had just gone to bed when he heard someone talking with his mother in a low voice. He got up and found that his father, who had been away for several days, was home. Ying Zheng hurried to embrace his father in excitement. His father hugged him back and said to his mother, "Qin's soldiers have already besieged the city of Handan. This evening Lyu Buwei will help me leave this place and return to Qin."

Hearing this, his mother was worried. "Aren't you a prince of Qin?" she said. "If Qin wages a war against Zhao, your life will be in danger."

His father managed a smile and said bitterly, "Qin is far away. No one there gives a dime about a hostage's life. I don't have time to talk any further. I need to go right away before it is too late."

His mother wept, "If you are gone, what will happen to the two of us? The King of Zhao will kill us. Please take us with you!"

Ying Yiren furrowed his brow and said, "It will draw attention and suspicion if the three of us flee together. I will leave first. Zhao won't harm you."

Hearing his father was leaving, Ying Zheng also became anxious. He held on to his father and said, "Daddy, I don't want you to go. Please don't leave us."

"Do you want me to stay here and die? Keep your voice low," Yiren said. "I don't want to be heard."

His father pushed away Ying Zheng's hands and left without turning back. Ying Zheng's eyes followed his father until he was out of sight. Holding onto his mother, Ying Zheng cried but still remembered to keep his voice low. As his father left and didn't bother to look back, he realized it was his mother who loved him most.

For some reason, the war didn't happen. Ying Zheng and his mother were safe, but his father never returned.

One day, Ying Zheng saw children playing with pebbles outside their gate. He found it interesting and asked, "May I join you to play?" A bigger child took a look at him and said, "OK." In a short while, smart Ying Zheng had won all the pebbles. The bigger child was not happy about this. He stood up in anger, grabbed Ying Zheng's pebbles and shoved him to the ground. "You are a hostage from Qin," he declared. "How can you win versus the people of Zhao? Brothers, come on, beat him!" The children listened to the bigger child, surrounded Ying Zheng and beat him.

Ying Zheng was hurt by the beating. He kept his eyes closed and used his arms to protect his head. He endured the beating without letting out a cry. Losing track of time, he heard a loud voice, "Stop, stop the beating!" He slowly opened his eyes and saw a well-dressed young man standing in front of him. Two tall soldiers followed the young man.

The bigger boy was intimidated by the soldiers but still tried to say loudly, "Who are you? We will beat whoever we want. It's none of your business."

A younger boy beside him whispered to him, "Brother, he is Dan, the crown prince of the State of Yan."

Hearing this, the bigger boy laughed, "Who cares if you're the crown prince of Yan or not. You are like Ying Zheng, a hostage kept by Zhao. Who do you think you are?"

Before he could finish his speech, the two soldiers rushed forward and seized him. Dan said to the soldiers, "Let him go. I just want to stop them."

The bigger child understood that they could not possibly beat the two soldiers and went away with his brothers.

From that time onwards, Ying Zheng and Prince Dan were good friends. As Yan was on good terms with Zhao, Prince Dan lived a comfortable life in Zhao. So he often helped Ying Zheng. Relations between Qin and Zhao, on the other hand, were on the decline. Ying Zheng and his mother had been ill treated. When he saw people bully him and his mother and curried favor with Dan, Ying Zheng would say to himself, "You are such snobs. Wait until father sends for me from Qin." But when would that be?

Three years passed but his father didn't send for him. Meanwhile, Prince Dan was preparing to return to the State of

Yan. On the evening before he left, Dan came to see Ying Zheng. He held Ying Zheng's hands in his and said, "I'm worried about you. How will your life be after I have gone? Without my protection, they may treat you even worse."

Something in his words made Ying Zheng rather uncomfortable. He pushed away Dan's hands and said, "Don't worry. My father will soon send people to escort me back to my country."

"Your father?" Dan laughed and said, "He is having a good time in Qin. He's left you behind. My guess is he never planned to come back for you."

Prince Dan left. Ying Zheng, standing by the gate, was stunned by the way his friend looked at him. Was it true that his father had left him behind for good? No, it couldn't be true. He would wait for his father to rescue him.

The days moved fast. Another three years passed. Finally, one day, his mother hurried into their home saying to Ying Zheng cheerfully, "Zheng, it is said that your father has become the crown prince of Qin and Lyu Buwei is now the Prime Minister of Qin. We can finally go to Qin!" Ying Zheng was thrilled by the news.

"Mother," he asked, "when will father send people for us?"

"I don't know," she replied, "but let's get prepared."

Two days flew by and they hadn't heard anything from his father. The King of Zhao, in order to please the future King of Qin, sent people to escort Ying Zheng and his mother to Qin. On the day of their departure, Ying Zheng coldly watched his mother happily collect their belongings and the neighbors who came to see them off. He kept reminding himself, "Father didn't send people for us. Instead, the King of Zhao offered to send us to Qin...." Ying Zheng, aged nine, left Handan where he was born and grew up.

Young Ruler

Ying Zheng eventually arrived in Qin. Within four years, his father died and Ying Zheng became the King of Qin at the age of 13. Ying Zheng was sorrowful because of his father's death. But now he was the King of Qin, and no one could domineer over him and his mother. He was capable of protecting his own mother. This thought comforted him and even made him proud of himself, but his pride didn't last long. Soon he realized his mother, the queen mother, and Lyu Buwei, the Counselor-in-Chief, were the de facto rulers. His orders did not carry much weight.

One day, Ying Zheng woke up early. He stood up and was about to summon servants when he overheard two maids whispering. "Did you know that last evening," one said, "the Counselor-in-Chief visited the queen mother's chamber again." "Don't you know that the queen mother was a maid of the Counselor-in-chief? They surely have a special relationship…" The other maid giggled.

Ying Zheng couldn't bear to hear more. He grabbed his sword hanging by his bed and rushed out. He killed the maid who was speaking. The other maid was terrified and ran towards the palace gate. Guards heard the noise and ran in to take away his sword.

"I am the King of Qin," Ying Zheng called out in a rage. "How dare you to take my sword?"

The guards withdrew and Ying Zheng was about to kill the other maid when Lyu Buwei walked in. "Stop!" he said. "Your Majesty, you cannot kill people at will! Guards, what are you waiting for?" Two guards quickly came forward and took away Ying Zheng's sword.

Ying Zheng was in shock. He laughed and said, "Good, good. The guards only obey the Counselor-in-Chief and not the King of Qin! You are the Counselor-in-Chief and my mother is the queen mother. You're on such good terms." With that, he went back to his room and didn't bother to see their reaction.

Lyu Buwei was surprised to hear Ying Zheng say these things, and didn't notice the queen mother's presence. "What happened?" she asked.

A maid answered in tears, "His Majesty got angry for no reason at all and killed one of us."

The queen mother smiled and said, "Only a maid. I thought something important had happened. Lyu, let's go." Lyu followed the queen mother out.

"Zheng seems to be aware of our relationship," he said to her.

The queen mother laughed. "He is still a child," she said. "Don't think too much of it. Let's go." From then on, Lyu seldom came around anymore. Ying Zheng gradually calmed down, but he found that he and his mother were now estranged.

One day, his mother said to him, "You're a grown man. It is not convenient for me to live in the palace any more. I want to move to Yongcheng City." Ying Zheng didn't want his mother to move away. However, he didn't want to displease her either. So he gave his consent. He didn't expect that after Lyu, his mother would live together with a man named Lao Ai. She moved away to keep him in the dark. Several years later, the queen mother and her lover had two children. Lao Ai accumulated more resources. He planned to kill Ying Zheng and enthrone his own son.

But Lao Ai's conspiracy didn't escape Ying Zheng's eyes and ears. Ying Zheng was already twenty years old and was preparing for the ceremony celebrating his adulthood. "Is the queen mother aware of this?" he asked the man who had told him about Lao's conspiracy.

The man lowered his head and took a while to summon his courage. "The queen mother already gave him the queen's jade seal," he said. "She told him to take advantage of the ceremony to seize the capital…"

"Ha ha!" Ying Zheng laughed maniacally, "Her Majesty even gave her seal to Lao Ai. Fine, I will be waiting for them."

Lao Ai's rebellion didn't stand a chance against Ying Zheng's well trained army. He was soon captured. Ying Zheng used the cruelest way the law stipulated to kill him. Ying Zheng could not kill his own mother so he placed her under house arrest in a palace. He didn't want to see her again. He also took his revenge against Lyu. He planned to keep Lyu in prison for a couple of years and then let him join Lao Ai in hell.

Ying Zheng, the King of Qin, had become a grown man in every respect. In the ceremony to mark his adulthood, he slowly put on his crown. "My father deserted me. My friend looked down upon me, even my mother betrayed me… On this vast land, who deserves my trust?" He took a sword and wore it on his waist. From then on, he always kept the sword by his side.

Founder of an Empire

Qin used to be the smallest and least powerful of the seven states during the Warring States Period. Located in the west of ancient China, its land was infertile and sparsely populated. People's lives were not easy. The kings of Qin were keen to develop its agriculture and military power. By the time Ying Zheng had ascended to the throne, Qin had become a powerful state.

For many years, wars and battles between states had been commonplace. It could be Qin attacking Wei (魏) and Zhao states, or the joint forces of Han, Wei (魏), Zhao, Wei (卫), or Chu states attacking Qin… Frequent wars changed Ying Zheng's perspectives and he became more composed and also more suspicious of others. He understood that in such times, if he spared another's life, he might be killed instead. If Qin did not conquer other states, it would be annihilated by others.

The growth of Qin could be greatly attributed to the proper use of talented people. Ying Zheng used different ways to recruit talents. Many talented people had been attracted and came to Qin. Qin became even more powerful. The kings of other states were certainly not happy about this situation.

One day, the king of Han said to his ministers, "Qin is growing stronger and stronger. We are Qin's nearest neighbor, Ying Zheng may attack us first. What can we do to prevent this from happening?"

Zheng Guo, one of the ministers, said, "Your Majesty, I have an idea. I will go to advise the king of Qin to build a canal. As Qin will need a lot of resources to build the canal, it won't wage wars. Then we will be safe." The king of Han was satisfied with this plan so he asked Zheng Guo to see Ying Zheng.

Ying Zheng heard Zheng Guo's advice and thought it was good for his country, so he mobilized hundreds of thousands of people to build the canal. The huge construction project demanded lots of hard work. Before it was completed, the secret plan of Zheng Guo and the king of Han was exposed as a plot to drain the resources of Qin and make it unable to wage wars. Ying Zheng was furious. He wanted to kill Zheng Guo and drive away talents from other states. Li Si, an official, wrote a letter to him, advising him not to do so. In the letter, Li Si stated if talents had been expelled, the power of Qin would diminish while other states would become stronger. Zheng Guo told Ying Zheng that although the canal was built to prevent Qin from attacking Han, once it was finished, it would benefit Qin greatly. Ying Zheng was persuaded. He did not expel talents from other states and let Zheng Guo continue to build the canal. Later, the canal was called the Zhengguo Canal and boosted the agriculture of Qin.

When Ying Zheng turned 30 years old, he began his plan to annex the other six states. Han, Qin's close neighbor, was the first. Then he led his army to the State of Zhao where he was born and spent the first several years of his life. He had mixed feelings towards this place. However, when his army reached Handan, Ying Zheng was already a hardened ruler. He killed his old enemies. How about his old friend? Ying Zheng did not have friends anymore. In order to protect the State of Yan, Prince Dan had sent an assassin named Jing Ke to kill Ying Zheng. Dan failed and he was executed by his own father. His severed head was sent to Qin as a friendly gesture. Looking at the head of his childhood friend, Ying Zheng remembered the day over twenty years before when the well-dressed Prince Dan helped him and drove away the bullies. But he could not remember when he had lost this friend. None of these things mattered anymore. Ying

Zheng understood that as the ruler of a state, he did not have the luxury of solid friendship; instead, he always had enemies. He had already annihilated Han and Zhao. He would conquer the rest one by one.

In 221 BC, Qin conquered Qi, the last surviving state, and unified ancient China. By then Ying Zheng was only 39 years old. He said to his ministers, "The alliance of Han, Zhao, and Wei attacked us. What happened to them? They were defeated. The king of Chu gave us his land and yet dared to attack us later. What happened to Chu? They were defeated. The crown prince of Yan sent Jing Ke to assassinate me. They failed and there is no more State of Yan. Qi used to be the most powerful state. It also fell. The title of king cannot match my achievements. I want a new title to let people remember me!"

The ministers looked at each other. No one dared say anything. "In ancient times, there was the Heavenly Huang (sovereign), the Earthly Huang, and the Tai Huang," an old minister said after quite a while. "The latter enjoyed the highest prestige. What about the title Tai Huang?"

Ying Zheng smiled. Looking at his ministers, he said, "In ancient times, there were three Huang and five Di (supreme ruler). They all had great achievements. But did any of them unify the country?" His remark took the ministers by surprise.

"No, they didn't," they replied. "Only you have unified the country."

Ying Zheng stood up and declared, "Even the three Huang and five Di cannot be compared to me. I will combine their titles and call myself Huang Di (the Emperor). I will be the First Emperor and my offspring will be the second, the third… the ten thousandth emperor. This title will pass through generations of my family." With that, Ying Zheng laughed heartily.

The ministers hurried to kneel down and said, "Yes, Your Majesty, long live the First Emperor! Long live the Qin Empire!"

"The land that belonged to Yan, Qi and Chu is too far away," one minister proposed several days later. "It is not easy to govern those places. You can assign princes to stay there and govern the places for you."

The Emperor did not express his opinion. He looked at the ministers and said, "What do you think of this proposal?"

The ministers discussed with each other in a low voice. "It has been common practice to let princes govern fiefdoms since ancient times," one of them said. "Otherwise, how is it possible to govern faraway places?"

Another echoed, "We should follow the established practice."

The Emperor coldly eyed his subjects and said, "That is indeed how things had been done. Then what happened? I become the Emperor, right?"

The ministers fell silent. Li Si looked at the Emperor and his fellow officials. He said, "If the fiefdoms are governed by sons and brothers of Your Majesty, connected by blood, the lords will stay in peace with each other for the time being. But in a few decades, they will become estranged. Some may even become enemies. There may be war between the fiefdoms. I suggest dividing the land into prefectures and counties, and assign officials to govern them. Princes will be given money instead of land. Without land, they won't have enough resources to betray

Your Majesty, and your empire will enjoy lasting peace and prosperity."

The Emperor smiled and said, "Good! That's exactly what I need. I will adopt Li Si's advice."

Therefore, the Emperor divided his empire into 36 prefectures which were governed by the central government. This two-tiered system had far-reaching influence in the following two thousand years.

The First Emperor was proud of this administrative reform, but he still felt that something was wrong. One morning, he summoned Li Si. "Li Si, I made my empire a more coherent state through establishing prefectures," the Emperor said. "However, people from the former Chu State still speak Chu dialect, write Chu script and use their former currency. So do people from the former State of Qi. Things like this still bother me. What's your opinion?"

Li Si lowered his head in thought. "Your Majesty, you have just raised an important point," he said. "If people still follow their local standards as before, we will run into lots of problems when governing the country and people will also constantly run into problems."

"Exactly," the Emperor said. "When my great-great-grandmother came to Qin from Chu, she went to buy some medicine prescribed by her home doctor. But the doctor in Qin couldn't read the prescription in Chu script and they didn't accept the currency of Chu either. She went through a lot of trouble to get the medicine. I am ruling the country as a whole. Yet, without a nationwide standard for script and currency, people won't have a sense of belonging to the Qin Empire."

Li Si replied, "A country is genuinely a coherent state with the same script and standardized units of measurements."

The Emperor laughed. "That's right," he said. "I will entrust you with this task."

From that point on, people in different places in the country wrote and read the same script. Even though they might speak with different accents, they could understand each other's writings, which led to better cultural exchanges. Trade became much easier when people used the same currency and followed the same weights and measures. The economy was boosted.

Death

The lives of the common people were getting better and people were benefiting from the unification and new systems. This did not change the fact that there were still some people who resented the First Emperor and the new systems. One day, soldiers arrested one man who was spreading a rumor that the Emperor was dying. The man was taken to the Emperor. "I heard that you were telling people that I will soon die," the Emperor said. "Why are you doing this?"

The man then looked at the Emperor straight in the eye and said, "You made such harsh laws and people are struggling to survive under your rule. I'm not the only one who wants you to die."

The ministers were terrified to hear this. "Long live the Emperor!" they said.

The man smiled and said, "Ha! No one can live forever. One day, you will die. And no one will remember you." Then he killed himself.

The man's last words got the Emperor's attention. He had unified the country and made such remarkable achievements, but he could not bear the thought that people would forget him in the future. He began to tour around his country to see his huge empire. Each place he went, he would set up a stele to record his achievements. He wanted everyone to know and remember him. One day a man named Xu Fu requested the Emperor's presence. "Your Majesty," Xu Fu proposed, "there are three heavenly mountains in the Eastern Sea where immortals reside. If I can find them, I will ask them for some elixir of life. Once Your Majesty takes the elixir, you will live forever."

The Emperor was more than happy to hear this. "Go and find me the elixir," he replied. "I will give you everything you need."

Xu Fu said with a smile, "I don't need much. I will take 1,500 boys and 1,500 girls to go with me by sea."

The Emperor got the ships ready for Xu Fu. Taking he people and money from the Emperor, Xu Fu set sail for the Eastern Sea.

A man named Lu Sheng heard about this and claimed also to be able to find the elixir of immortality. The First Emperor was pleased and gave him lots of money for the mission. Lu Sheng told the Emperor that he had read an ancient sacred book which said the Qin Empire would be overthrown by Xiongnu, a nomadic ethnic group from the north. The Emperor couldn't bear the thought that the empire he built would be taken over by Xiongnu. He sent General Meng Tian with an army of over 300,000 people to the north to fight them and mobilized countless people to build the Great Wall to guard agaist their attack. It was a difficult project. Nearly 100,000 people died during its construction. However, in the coming years, the Great Wall proved to be an important fortification for guarding the country, allowing people south of the Great Wall to be less troubled by raids and attacks.

Several years later, some scholars began to criticize the new systems and praise the older ones. Li Si said to the First Emperor, "Your achievements have already surpassed all rulers in the past. Those scholars are pedants who know nothing other than how to recite books. We'd better burn the books of the former states and keep only the books of Qin and monographs on medical studies and agriculture. Then no one can speak ill of the new systems." The Emperor gave his consent.

Xu Fu went on his journey to seek the immortals but never returned. Lu Sheng, who went to find the elixir of immortality, also fled. The Emperor was enraged. These futile missions cost him tremendous amounts of money, and he felt betrayed and humiliated. He sent his men to arrest those who had deceived him or spoke against him, and buried them alive. Fusu, his eldest son, said to him, "Your Empire has just settled in peace. If Your Majesty implement such harsh laws, your people may turn against you." His words displeased the Emperor and he sent him away to live in the far north.

Fusu's words may not have been pleasant, but they were true. More and more people wished the death of the Emperor. On the Emperor's third tour seeing his empire, an assassin attacked him in today's Yuanyang County, Henan Province. A big iron hammer hit one of the carriages and killed all the passengers. Luckily, the Emperor was riding in another carriage and survived. Not long after that, someone claimed to have found a meteor with an inscription that had fallen from the sky. The inscription said, "Death to the First Emperor." People were saying that heaven was angry and wanted the First Emperor to die. The Emperor certainly did not believe that. He believed that someone had carved the inscription. He arrested people in the neighborhood where the stone was found and wanted to find the people responsible for it. But no one had any answers. In the end, the Emperor killed all of them. Not long after that, one minister was told by a passer-by, "Please pass my words to the Emperor: This year the first dragon will die." The passer-by disappeared right after this was said. The Emperor usually never believed stories like this, but this time, he was speechless for quite a while before he finally said, "The first dragon must refer to me."

The First Emperor was quite aware of his declining health. He would have to pass on his empire to one of his sons eventually. During his fifth tour, he was seriously ill. He wrote a letter to Fusu, saying, "I'm dying. Return to Xianyang. You will be the emperor after I pass away." This letter wasn't delivered. Zhao Gao, a minister, intercepted it. Zhao Gao used to be the teacher of Huhai, the Emperor's another son. He wanted Huhai to be the next emperor. The First Emperor of Qin died on a summer day in Shaqiu, in present-day Xingtai City, Hebei Province. Li Si kept it secret to prevent possible rebellions. Only a few people knew the Emperor was dead. To disguise this fact, food was delivered to the Emperor's carriage as usual. Zhao Gao and Li Si burned the letter to Fusu and forged another one asking Fusu and General Meng Tian to commit suicide. Once again, Fusu and Meng Tian obeyed "the Emperor's" order.

It was the hottest time of year. The body of the Emperor began to stink. To cover this, Li Si and Zhao Gao put stinky dry fish onto every carriage. People could detect the stink when they passed by the carriages but couldn't tell what it was. Li Si declared the First Emperor's death after they arrived in Xianyang. Huhai became the Second Emperor of Qin. He ruled the country with even more cruelty, more than the people could bear. Rebellions broke out throughout the country. The Qin Empire, despite the great aspirations of the First Emperor, was a short lived empire.

People of the following generations remembered the First Emperor's cruelty. Nevertheless, he was one of the most influential statesmen and reformers in China's history. He, for the first time, made ancient China a unified country in a real sense, with standardized script, weights and measures… The Qin Dynasty lived for only 15 years, but the centralized administration system headed by the emperor remained the core of China's governing system for over two thousand years. With standard writing, Chinese people of different ethnic groups are able to communicate with each other. The Great Wall protected central China from attacks of nomadic tribes, and nowadays it is still considered a Wonder of the World. The First Emperor of Qin's influence on China has never ceased.

练习题

一、选择题。Choose the correct answer.

1. 秦始皇出生在哪一年？（　　）

   A. 公元 259 年　　　　B. 公元 256 年

   C. 公元前 259 年　　　D. 公元前 256 年

2. 秦始皇的父亲是（　　）。

   A. 赵国的国王　　　　B. 韩国的王子

   C. 秦国的太子　　　　D. 秦国太子的儿子

3. 嬴政被几个赵国小孩子痛打，帮助他的是（　　）。

   A. 秦国太子　　　　　B. 赵国太子

   C. 燕国太子　　　　　D. 妈妈

4. 举行成人礼的时候，嬴政是（　　）。

   A. 十三岁　　　　　　B. 二十岁

   C. 三十岁　　　　　　D. 三十九岁

5. 嬴政认为身边可以信任的人是（　　）。

   A. 父亲　　　　　　　B. 朋友

   C. 母亲　　　　　　　D. 没有人

6. 嬴政重用的人是（　　）。

   A. 贵族　　　　　　　B. 百姓

C. 兄弟　　　　　　　　D. 真正的人才

7. 建议嬴政修建水渠的是（　　）。

　　A. 大臣郑国　　　　　B. 郑国人

　　C. 韩王　　　　　　　D. 李斯

8. 韩王担心秦国第一个攻打韩国，是因为（　　）。

　　A. 在六国中韩国最强大

　　B. 在六国中韩国离秦国最近

　　C. 嬴政在韩国当过人质

　　D. 嬴政最不喜欢韩王

9. 李斯说赶走人才，会（　　）。

　　A. 让秦国自己的力量变小

　　B. 带来更多的敌人

　　C. 让别的国家更强大

　　D. 以上都对

10. 第一个统一中国的人是（　　）。

　　A. 天皇　　　　　　　B. 地皇

　　C. 泰皇　　　　　　　D. 秦始皇

11. 燕国、齐国很远，秦始皇管理这些地方的办法是（　　）。

　　A. 派儿子去管理　　　B. 派兄弟去管理

　　C. 派李斯去管理　　　D. 设立郡县，统一管理

12. 秦始皇把国家分成（　　）个郡县。

　　A. 十三　　　　　　B. 三十

　　C. 三十六　　　　　D. 三十九

13. 下面哪项内容不是秦始皇统一的？（　　）

　　A. 统一文字　　　　B. 统一语言

　　C. 统一钱币　　　　D. 统一度量衡

14. 秦始皇到处巡游是为了（　　）。

　　A. 管理六国　　　　B. 找到仙人

　　C. 让人们记住他　　D. 抓住刺客

15. 李斯建议秦始皇烧了哪些书？（　　）

　　A. 秦国的书　　　　B. 其他国家的书

　　C. 医学的书　　　　D. 农学的书

16. 秦始皇把大儿子扶苏赶走，是因为（　　）。

　　A. 扶苏没有找到长生不老药

　　B. 扶苏欺骗了他

　　C. 扶苏让他很生气

　　D. 扶苏想去修建长城

17. 秦始皇死在了（　　）。

　　A. 咸阳　　　　　　B. 邯郸

　　C. 沙丘平台　　　　D. 第五次巡游的路上

18. 李斯没有对外说出秦始皇死了，是因为（　　）。

　　A. 担心有人会叛乱　　B. 想让扶苏做皇帝

　　C. 想让胡亥做皇帝　　D. 自己想做皇帝

19. 李斯和赵高在秦始皇的车上放鲍鱼是因为（　　）。

　　A. 鲍鱼很多　　　　　B. 鲍鱼很贵

　　C. 鲍鱼很臭　　　　　D. 鲍鱼很好吃

20. 以下哪件事不是秦始皇做的？（　　）

　　A. 完成了中国的统一　B. 建立了皇帝制度

　　C. 统一了文字　　　　D. 找到了长生不老药

二、判断题：请根据故事内容判断下列说法是否正确，如果正确请标"T"，不正确请标"F"。
Decide whether the following statements are true (T) or false (F).

1. 嬴政出生在秦国。　　　　　　　　　　　　（　　）

2. 嬴政一出生就成为赵国的人质。　　　　　　（　　）

3. 为了嬴异人一家的安全，秦国没有和赵国打仗。（　　）

4. 太子丹比嬴政先离开赵国。　　　　　　　　（　　）

5. 嬴政的父亲成为太子以后，马上就派人接嬴政回秦国。

　　　　　　　　　　　　　　　　　　　　　（　　）

6. 太后不知道嫪毐要叛乱的事。　　　　　　　（　　）

7. 嬴政当上秦王的时候，秦国是七国中最小最穷的国家。

（　　）

8. 修建"郑国渠"给秦国的农业带来了好处。（　　）
9. 郡县制度从秦始皇开始，在中国沿用了两千年。（　　）
10. 徐福告诉秦始皇，秦会被匈奴消灭。（　　）
11. 秦始皇派人把欺骗自己和反对自己的人活埋了。（　　）
12. 因为担心扶苏和蒙恬叛乱，秦始皇写信让他们自杀。

（　　）

13. 秦始皇死的时候是冬天。（　　）
14. 很多人认为秦始皇是一个残暴的皇帝。（　　）
15. 秦始皇对中国历史的影响很大。（　　）

三、选择填空。Choose the appropriate words to fill in the parentheses.

1. 父亲（　　）开嬴政的手，头也不回地（　　）了。（　　）着远去的父亲，嬴政（　　）着母亲，小声地（　　）了起来。父亲看都不看他就走了，只有母亲是最爱他的。

A. 望　　B. 哭　　C. 推　　D. 抱　　E. 走

2. 嬴政慢慢戴上了王冠，"我的父亲（　　）我，我的朋友（　　）我，就连母亲也（　　）了我……这天下，还有谁是可以（　　）的?"他拿起一把剑,把它挂在身上,从那以后,这把剑就天天陪伴着他。

  A. 背叛 B. 抛弃 C. 信任 D. 看不起

3. 一天早上,他把李斯找来,对他说:"李斯,郡县制度（　　）建立了,（　　）楚地的人还是说楚国的话,写楚国的字,用楚国的钱;齐地的人（　　）说齐国的话,写齐国的字,用齐国的钱。我觉得有什么地方不对。你怎么看?"

  A. 可是 B. 还是 C. 虽然

4. 有个叫徐福的人来对秦始皇说:"皇上,东海有三座（　　）,那里住着（　　）,如果找到他们,问他们要一些（　　）,您吃了就能永远不老、不死。"

  A. 仙药 B. 仙人 C. 仙山

5. 秦始皇非常（　　）,这些人（　　）了他那么多的钱,到头来却还是（　　）了他! 于是,他派人把那些（　　）和反对他的人都抓起来,把他们全都活埋了。秦始皇的大儿子扶苏说:"天下刚刚安定,您的法律这样严厉,百姓们恐怕要（　　）您了。"

  A. 背叛 B. 欺骗 C. 反对 D. 生气 E. 拿

四、连线题。 Match.

1. 请把下列人物与他们的职务连起来。

   A. 嬴政　　　　　a. 秦国太后
   B. 嬴政的母亲　　b. 秦国相国
   C. 吕不韦　　　　c. 秦国国王
   D. 李斯　　　　　d. 秦国大臣

2. 下列人物和嬴政是什么关系？请连线。

   A. 嬴异人　　　　a. 嬴政的父亲
   B. 赵高　　　　　b. 嬴政的朋友
   C. 太子丹　　　　c. 嬴政的儿子
   D. 胡亥　　　　　d. 嬴政的大臣

3. 下列人物对嬴政做过什么事？请连线。

   A. 李斯　　　　　a. 派刺客刺杀秦始皇
   B. 赵高　　　　　b. 拿走了秦始皇写给扶苏的信
   C. 扶苏　　　　　c. 不告诉人们秦始皇已经死了
   D. 太子丹　　　　d. 批评秦始皇的法律太严厉

五、请根据故事内容给下列句子排列顺序。
Put the following statements in order according to the story.

1. 下列事件发生的先后顺序是_____。

   A. 嬴政外出巡游

   B. 嬴政统一文字、钱和度量衡

   C. 嬴政吞并六国

   D. 嬴政称"始皇帝"

2. 嬴政吞并下面几个国家的顺序是_____。

   A. 赵国　　B. 齐国　　C. 韩国　　D. 燕国

3. 下列事件发生的先后顺序是_____。

   A. 有人发现了韩王和郑国的秘密

   B. 韩王害怕秦国攻打韩国

   C. 李斯写了一篇文章,请嬴政不要赶走人才

   D. 郑国建议嬴政修建水渠

   E. 嬴政要赶走外来的人才

   F. 秦国的农业发展得更好

   G. 郑国继续修建水渠

六、图片题。Answer the following questions according to the picture.

1. 图中帮助嬴政的人是谁？他是嬴政真正的朋友吗？

2. 嬴政和母亲终于能够回秦国了，可是为什么嬴政看起来不太高兴？

3. 结合图片和书中的描写，说说嬴政为什么会越来越冷酷。

4. 请你说说这幅图中发生的故事，以及人物的心理活动。

七、思考题。Answer the following question according to the story.

1. 评价秦始皇的功与过，请举出实例证明自己的看法。

2. 如果你生活在战国时代，你想成为一个什么样的人？

练习题答案 Keys to the exercises

一、选择题
1. C 2. D 3. C 4. B 5. D
6. D 7. A 8. B 9. D 10. D
11. D 12. C 13. B 14. C 15. B
16. C 17. C 18. A 19. C 20. D

二、判断题：请根据故事内容判断下列说法是否正确，如果正确请标"T"，不正确请标"F"
1. F 2. T 3. F 4. T 5. F
6. F 7. F 8. T 9. T 10. F
11. T 12. F 13. F 14. T 15. T

三、选择填空
1. C E A D B
2. B D A C
3. C A B
4. C B A
5. D E A B C

四、连线题
1. A-c B-a C-b D-d
2. A-a B-d C-b D-c
3. A-c B-b C-d D-a

五、请根据故事内容给下列句子排列顺序
　　1. C-D-B-A
　　2. C-A-D-B
　　3. B-D-A-E-C-G-F

六、图片题
　　（答案略）

七、思考题
　　（答案略）

词汇表
Vocabulary List

安定	adj.	āndìng	stable, settled
霸业	n.	bàyè	hegemony
鲍鱼	n.	bàoyú	stinky fish (in ancient time), abalone (now)
碑	n.	bēi	stele
背叛	v.	bèipàn	betray
闭	v.	bì	close, shut
残暴	adj.	cánbào	cruel, ruthless
称	v.	chēng	call, name
成人礼	n.	chéngrénlǐ	coming-of-age ceremony
冲	v.	chōng	charge, dash
重新	adv.	chóngxīn	again, anew
仇人	n.	chóurén	foe, enemy
臭味	n.	chòuwèi	stench, foul odor
传①	v.	chuán	pass on
传②	v.	chuán	transmit, spread
刺客	n.	cìkè	assassin
打败	v.	dǎbài	defeat
打仗	v.	dǎzhàng	fight, go to war
大臣	n.	dàchén	minister
抵挡	v.	dǐdǎng	keep off, ward off, withstand
都城	n.	dūchéng	capital
度量衡	n.	dùliànghéng	weights and measures
法律	n.	fǎlǜ	law
反抗	v.	fǎnkàng	fight against, rebel against, resist
疯	adj.	fēng	mad, insane
否认	v.	fǒurèn	deny
改革家	n.	gǎigéjiā	reformer
高祖母	n.	gāozǔmǔ	(paternal) great-great-grandmother
更改	v.	gēnggǎi	change, alter
公元	n.	gōngyuán	Christian era
公子	n.	gōngzǐ	son of a prince, official or a rich man

功业	n.	gōngyè	outstanding achievements
攻	v.	gōng	attack
宫女	n.	gōngnǚ	palace maid
古代	n.	gǔdài	ancient times
挂	v.	guà	hang up
管理	v.	guǎnlǐ	manage, run
跪	v.	guì	kneel
国王	n.	guówáng	king
恨	v.	hèn	hate
华丽	adj.	huálì	magnificent, gorgeous
皇帝	n.	huángdì	emperor
嫁	v.	jià	(of a woman) marry
建立	v.	jiànlì	establish, found
剑	n.	jiàn	sword
焦急	adj.	jiāojí	anxious, worried
接	v.	jiē	meet, pick up
经济	n.	jīngjì	economy
军事	n.	jūnshì	military affairs
君主	n.	jūnzhǔ	monarch
郡县	n.	jùnxiàn	prefecture and county
刻	v.	kè	carve
口音	n.	kǒuyīn	accent
冷酷	adj.	lěngkù	callous
愣	v.	lèng	be dumbfounded
力量	n.	lìliàng	strength, power
历史	n.	lìshǐ	history
另	pron.	lìng	other, another
秘密	n.	mìmì	secret
民族	n.	mínzú	nation, ethnic group
名号	n.	mínghào	name, title
纽带	n.	niǔdài	bond, link
农学	n.	nóngxué	agricultural sciences
农业	n.	nóngyè	agriculture
派	v.	pài	send, dispatch
抛弃	v.	pāoqì	abandon, desert
篇	m.w.	piān	(for paper, articles, etc.) sheet, piece

贫瘠	adj.	pínjí	infertile, poor
欺负	v.	qīfu	bully
欺骗	v.	qīpiàn	deceive, cheat
奇迹	n.	qíjì	miracle, wonder
强大	adj.	qiángdà	powerful
抢	v.	qiǎng	grab, rob
穷	adj.	qióng	poor
权势	n.	quánshì	power and influence
人质	n.	rénzhì	hostage
烧	v.	shāo	burn
身边	n.	shēnbiān	one's side/vicinity
身份	n.	shēnfèn	identity, status
尸体	n.	shītǐ	corpse
石头	n.	shítou	stone
时期	n.	shíqī	period
士兵	n.	shìbīng	soldier
书同文，车同轨		shū tóng wén, chē tóng guǐ	standardize script and the width between wheels, a phrase used as a metaphor for the unification of a country
疏远	adj.	shūyuǎn	be estranged from
水渠	n.	shuǐqú	canal
顺畅	adj.	shùnchàng	smooth
随便	adj.	suíbiàn	casual, random
讨好	v.	tǎohǎo	curry favor with
提心吊胆		tíxīn-diàodǎn	have one's heart in one's mouth
铁锤	n.	tiěchuí	iron hammer
停止	v.	tíngzhǐ	stop, cease
童年	n.	tóngnián	childhood
统一	v.	tǒngyī	unify
土地	n.	tǔdì	land, terrain
推	v.	tuī	push
王冠	n.	wángguān	crown
王子	n.	wángzǐ	prince
围	v.	wéi	enclose, surround
伟大	adj.	wěidà	great
文字	n.	wénzì	script, writing

吓	v.	xià	frighten
仙	n.	xiān	immortal
咸阳	pn.	Xiányáng	Xianyang (capital of the Qin Dynasty)
相国	n.	xiàngguó	Counselor-in-Chief
消灭	v.	xiāomiè	eliminate
小院	n.	xiǎo yuàn	small courtyard
信任	v.	xìnrèn	trust
兄弟	n.	xiōngdì	brothers
匈奴	n.	Xiōngnú	Xiongnu
修建	v.	xiūjiàn	build, construct
修筑	v.	xiūzhù	build, construct
巡游	v.	xúnyóu	travel around, patrol
严厉	adj.	yánlì	strict, harsh
沿用	v.	yányòng	continue to use
药方	n.	yàofāng	prescription
医学	n.	yīxué	medical science
议论	v.	yìlùn	discuss, talk about
赢	v.	yíng	win
影响	v.	yǐngxiǎng	influence
玉玺	n.	yùxǐ	imperial jade seal
战国	n.	Zhànguó	Warring States (475-221BC)
战争	n.	zhànzhēng	war
招收	v.	zhāoshōu	recruit
睁	v.	zhēng	open (eyes)
政治家	n.	zhèngzhìjiā	statesman
制度	n.	zhìdù	system, institution
中央	n.	zhōngyāng	central government, center
皱眉头	v.	zhòu méitóu	frown
著名	adj.	zhùmíng	famous, celebrated
抓	v.	zhuā	grab, seize
自杀	v.	zìshā	commit suicide
尊贵	adj.	zūnguì	honorable, respected

项目策划：刘小琳　韩　颖
责任编辑：韩　颖　付　眉
英文编辑：薛彧威
英文审定：黄长奇　James Hutchison
插图绘制：赵倩倩
封面设计：E·T创意工作室

图书在版编目（CIP）数据

秦始皇 / 叶婵娟改编. -- 北京：华语教学出版社，2017.6
（"彩虹桥"汉语分级读物．3级：750词）
ISBN 978-7-5138-1401-0

Ⅰ．①秦… Ⅱ．①叶… Ⅲ．①汉语－对外汉语教学－语言读物 Ⅳ．① H195.5

中国版本图书馆CIP数据核字（2017）第144378号

秦始皇

叶婵娟　改编
张　乐　翻译
*
©华语教学出版社有限责任公司
华语教学出版社有限责任公司出版
（中国北京百万庄大街24号　邮政编码 100037）
电话：(86)10-68320585　68997826
传真：(86)10-68997826　68326333
网址：www.sinolingua.com.cn
电子信箱：hyjx@sinolingua.com.cn
北京虎彩文化传播有限公司印刷
2017年（32开）第1版
2022年第1版第2次印刷
（汉英）
ISBN 978-7-5138-1401-0
002500